THE BITTER HERBS

*5 short plays of Jewish life in America
for the Passover Season*

THE BITTER HERBS

*5 short plays of Jewish life in America
for the Passover Season*

By

Mark Troy

THE MISGUIDED PRODUCTION
THE PLOT
HOOD RATZ
THE BASIC 7
JOIN THE CLUB

TINSEL ROAD BOOKS

THE BITTER HERBS

ISBN: 978-0-981943-11-4

Library of Congress Cataloging-in-Publication-Data is available on file. Library of Congress Control Number: 2009902038

Published by Tinsel Road Books
171 Pier Avenue, #328
Santa Monica, California 90405 USA
www.tinselroad.com

Tinsel Road Books, in association with Global ReLeaf, will plant two trees for each tree used in the manufacturing of this book. Global ReLeaf is an international campaign by American Forests, the nation's oldest nonprofit conservation organization and a world leader in planting trees for environmental restoration.

Produced by SST Productions in association with Kurt J. Swanson,
Bitter Herbs originally opened at the Sidewalk Studio Theatre,
Toluca Lake, CA. on the evening of March 21 2009.

For Coco. Everyday.

The Bitter Herbs opened at the Sidewalk Studio Theatre, Toluca Lake, CA. on the evening of March 21, 2009. It was directed by Sal Romeo. Produced by SST Productions, Inc. in association with Kurt J. Swanson. Sets by Marc W. Haupert. Lighting: Rebecca Bonebrake, Costumes: Jessica Kilzer, Stage Manager: Becky Harrison, Associate Producers: Jessica Kilzer, Eddie Chern. It had the following cast in order of appearance:

THE MISGUIDED PRODUCTION

Characters

YONKLE SCHWARTZBAUM.......   **Danny Lippin**

BECKY MIZRAHI........................   **Nickella Moschetti**

A living room in Park Slope, Brooklyn, New York

THE PLOT

Characters

EFFIE...   **Colette Freedman**

DESDEMONA..............................   **Sharon Madden**

A living room in the East Village, New York

HOOD RATZ

Characters

BEN KATZ...................................   **Michael Shaw**

ARTHUR KATZ...........................   **Danny Lippin**

SALLY PEABODY......................   **Colette Freedman**

YEWANDE.................................   **Malcolm Devine**

A living room in the Fairfax District of Los Angeles

THE BASIC 7

Characters

BART BROMBERG………………..	**Michael Shaw**
SHEILA BROMBERG…………….	**Nickella Moschetti**

A living room in Sherman Oaks, California

JOIN THE CLUB

Characters

ESTHER ZULMAN………….......	**Colette Freedman**
BOBBY O'MALLEY……………….	**Danny Lippin**
RABBI MEYERS……………………..	**Michael Shaw**
FATHER DEMITRIE……………….	**Malcolm Devine**

A living room in Santa Monica, California

*understudies: Bryan Richard Deehring, Francesca Ferrara, Michael Patrick McGill

Author's Note: The Bitter Herbs, the collection of short plays gathered here have been performed separately, and of course, can be in the future. For this collection, and this production, the plays should all take place in the same living room set, and with brief song choices to separate the action of each piece. The only difference to the set would be a small change; a picture, a box of matzoh, some wine glasses, etc.

It should be performed without Intermission.

The Bitter Herbs

THE MISGUIDED PRODUCTION

RABBI SCHWARTZBAUM'S house. A young RABBI YONKLE SCHWARTZBAUM, late 30s, good looking, in suit and tie with small hand-knit yalmuka on, stares at BECKY MIZRAHI seated on the sofa. SHE is young, effervescent, and dressed in button-down blouse and short skirt.

RABBI SCHWARTZBAUM. I'm afraid I'm going to have insist upon the nudity.

BECKY. I... I really don't feel comfortable with that (*Adding*)
Rabbi Schwartzbaum.

RABBI SCHWARTZBAUM. *Dahling. Dahling*, I understand where you're coming from, my dear. But you're not seeing the whole picture. The whole religious and political picture. Look at me. Would it surprise you to know that I was a stand-in for a young Tom Cruise in a little picture called "Days of Thunder?"

BECKY. (*Impressed*) You know Tom Cruise?

RABBI SCHWARTZBAUM. A very nice Jewish boy.

BECKY. Tom Cruise isn't Jewish.

RABBI SCHWARTZBAUM. We didn't spend much time together... work work work, you know how a movie set is.

BECKY. I have no idea how a movie set is.

RABBI SCHWARTZBAUM. My point is, I am fully aware of the types of hardships and "glass ceilings" one comes across in the entertainment field as much as you are.

BECKY. I'm not aware of any of that, Rabbi.

RABBI SCHWARTZBAUM. Would it surprise you to know that for a short time while I was looking to reign as a temple rabbi I worked six days a week and seven nights in the mail room at The William Morris Agency?

BECKY. That's impressive, right?

RABBI SCHWARTZBAUM. Mr. Morris and I were as close as two men could be without tongue kissing.

BECKY. Mr. Morris. Isn't he like dead a hundred years?

RABBI SCHWARTZBAUM. I was busy sorting mail, I didn't pay much attention to the daily goings on. Work work work. My point is, I know what I'm talking about. I know how these things are done. I know without a shadow of a doubt that this part definitely calls for nudity.

BECKY. But, Rabbi Schwartzbaum... you're doing "Fiddler On The Roof."

RABBI SCHWARTZBAUM. Yes. Yes. That's my very point. "Fiddler On The Roof." Would it surprise you to know that I happen to know a lot about show business?

BECKY. At this point. Yes, it would surprise me to know you happen to know a lot about show business.

RABBI SCHWARTZBAUM. I have no intention of scaring you, Becky. I am a virtuous man. A clean thinking, pious person. Ask Susan Sarandon who I was a stunt double for in her remarkable role in "Thelma & Louise."

BECKY. You were a stunt double for Susan Sarandon?

RABBI SCHWARTZBAUM. Another life, another time. Let's talk about the business at hand. The business of me as a qualified theatrical director.

BECKY. Yes. About the nudity. Is it total nudity?

RABBI SCHWARTZBAUM. Is there any other kind? Let me see if I can explain this. *(Paces; HER eyes on HIM)* Since the sixties... since Zero Mostel, everybody... EVERYBODY has been doing the great Sholom Aleichem story... the Jules Stein musical "Fiddler On The Roof" the same way. The exact same way. Curtain up: a fiddler sits on the roof. Pathetic. *(Humming opening music)* Dum dum dumdumdumdum...doy doy doy doy doy doy... la la la la la la... the same old stupid thing. The five daughters are introduced. The milkman sings "Tradition," we meet Motel-the-tailor, the next thing you know Tzeitel is engaged. They sing "To Life," they drink, there's a wedding. The point is -- the Cossacks come in, the Jews go out, the curtain comes down, the show is over. You're having a corned beef on rye at the Second Avenue deli and you've spent three hundred dollars and nobody's the wiser. Do you get my point, Becky?

BECKY. I do not get your point, Rabbi.

RABBI SCHWARTZBAUM. Where's the originality? Where's the passion for story? Where's the director's touch?

BECKY. You have it?

RABBI SCHWARTZBAUM. I have it, Becky. Lord knows I have it. It's written all over my face. And in my short production notes.

(HE pulls out a HUGE "directors book")

BECKY. Looks like you've done your homework.

RABBI SCHWARTZBAUM. I've been working on this project since my Bar Mitzvah. Do you know what that's like, Becky?

BECKY. I have no idea what that's like, Rabbi.

RABBI SCHWARTZBAUM. I have ideas. I have plans. You've heard of Stanley Kubrick? You've heard of Martin Scorcese? You've heard of Sidney Pollack? I'm none of them. I could be bigger!

BECKY. Those are film directors. You're doing a stage play.

RABBI SCHWARTZBAUM. I'm starting in the theater. Starting. Before long the theater won't be able to afford me, and I'll spit on it.

BECKY. You'll spit on the theater?

RABBI SCHWARTZBAUM. *(HE spits)* Everybody does. Becky, someday the Directors Guild of America will be giving out the Rabbi Schwartzbaum Memorial Fund Award to young up-and-coming junior rabbinical students who also enjoy making short films.

BECKY. Now I'm impressed!

RABBI SCHWARTZBAUM. Would it surprise you to know that while I was in Rabbinical Seminary school, when I first noticed my grades slipping, I directed myself in a fabulously smashing production of "Show Boat?" Sold out three performances. Ran over four days! There I was singing "Old Man River..." *(HE does a few bars)* to a room full of German S.S. Officers.

BECKY. Isn't that "Cabaret?"

RABBI SCHWARTZBAUM. There are German S.S. Officers in "Cabaret?"

BECKY. I don't go to the theater much, but I think --

RABBI SCHWARTZBAUM. We musta done some rewriting -- you gonna report me to the Dramatist Guild? It was a hit! I tell you! A hit.

BECKY. But Rabbi Schwartzbaum, this is an amateur production.

RABBI SCHWARTZBAUM. Amateur! You call my production amateur?! When I was working as a junior rabbi in a small conservative temple on the lower East Side, when I first noticed my constituents falling asleep during the morning service, I told myself that no matter how few production values a show of mine might have... I would treat each and every aspect of that show as if it was on Broadway! Broadway!

BECKY. But people will be eating.

RABBI SCHWARTZBAUM. EATING?! People are eating during my show?

What are they theatrical snobs? Vagrants? Second act sneak-in's.

BECKY. No, Rabbi Schwartzbaum, they're eating because they serve food. The theater is in the basement of the temple. They serve dinner while the show is on.

RABBI SCHWARTZBAUM. I'm directing dinner theater? Oh God. Look at my career. Look what's happened to my career?

BECKY. You're talking about your rabbinical career?

RABBI SCHWARTZBAUM. No. My career as a qualified theatrical director. When I got my own temple -- when I first noticed people didn't take me seriously and giggled during my speeches -- I never thought I'd be directing dinner theater. It's so Vegas.

BECKY. Everyone has to start someplace.

RABBI SCHWARTZBAUM. But I'm at the top of my game!

BECKY. Actually you're at the bottom of your game.

RABBI SCHWARTZBAUM. Yes. But I'm at the very top of the very bottom of my game! *(Broken-hearted)* Dinner theater... Next thing you know they'll make me use Paul Anka in the role of Tevya.

BECKY. They won't make you use Paul Anka in the role of Tevya.

RABBI SCHWARTZBAUM. Thank you for respecting me, Becky.

BECKY. I hear they got Steven Seagal,

RABBI SCHWARTZBAUM. *(Jumps up) SEAGAL?!* I'm calling my agent. I'm calling that scum-bag idiot shyster moron of an agent and I am going to tell him I've moving on. I'm seeking newer representation. I'm going to a boutique agency.

BECKY. But why were you with him, Rabbi, if he was such a scum-bag idiot shyster moron of an agent?

RABBI SCHWARTZBAUM. He took my calls. You think it's easy finding representation?

BECKY. I have no idea --

RABBI SCHWARTZBAUM. -- To be frank, Becky, I'm working with a manager-type. Agents are very difficult to sign with. You'll see. You'll see. When it's your turn to write the letters and go for the interviews... each day it will break your heart.

BECKY. I don't want an agent, Rabbi Schwartzbaum.

RABBI SCHWARTZBAUM. Everyone wants an agent.

BECKY. But I'm not in show business.

RABBI SCHWARTZBAUM. Did this stop The Hilton Sisters? All right! Okay. God you're good at this. I'm being piggy-backed by a commercial agency who does have some eight-by-ten glossies of close-ups I took from my trip to Colorado last summer. I'm not technically signed with anyone. Yes. This is my first show here at Sinai Temple of The East Side, and I thank you for coming to my home today, but things are going to change at the temple now that I'm here -- I can assure you that, Miss Mizrahi, I can assure you that things will change.

BECKY. I don't want people eating while I sing, Rabbi. And I certainly don't want people eating while I sing naked. What if someone coughs on a piece of fish or something? That could screw up my timing.

RABBI SCHWARTZBAUM. I'm talking "art" here, Becky. The opportunity to bring to the stage a new vision of "Fiddler" never before seen.

BECKY. I don't go to musicals much. I like television.

RABBI SCHWARTZBAUM. *(Grabs HIS heart)* Oh dear Moses. We're going to see a show. Immediately. We're going to see lots of shows. We're going to start with the musical "Annie" and work our way all the way up to "Urinetown."

BECKY. That's disgusting.

RABBI SCHWARTZBAUM. You haven't seen it yet.

BECKY. *(Happily)* Are you asking me out, on a date?

RABBI SCHWARTZBAUM. Out? No. Yes. Yes. We're friends, right?

BECKY. *(Disappointed)* I suppose.

RABBI SCHWARTZBAUM. I know how to get tickets to any show on Broadway you'd like. My agent picks up the phone and makes one call... Oh damn. I can't call today. He doesn't like when I call more than fourteen times a day and I've already exceeded my limit for the week.

BECKY. Thank you for thinking of me, Rabbi Schwartzbaum.

RABBI SCHWARTZBAUM. There's a whole world out there, Becky. You should see it. It's a world full of energy, passion, and life full of music and song.

BECKY. And you'll show it to me?

RABBI SCHWARTZBAUM. I'll...

(THEIR eyes meet but both break the moment)

RABBI SCHWARTZBAUM. Becky. I'm tired of moving my lips along to shows I've seen a hundred times done the same way. Let me show you something that will change the face of American Jewish theater!

BECKY. You're beautiful, Rabbi Schwartzbaum when you talk show biz.

RABBI SCHWARTZBAUM. Am I? Do you know why they do the same old thing, Miss Mizrahi? The same old five daughters introduced, milkman sings "Tradition," meet Motel, Tzeitel engaged, sing "To Life," have a wedding, Cossacks come, Jews go, curtain down?

BECKY. Does it have something to do with Actor's Equity?

RABBI SCHWARTZBAUM. Well…yeah. No. It has something to do with having no foresight. We have to go with the nudity, Becky, because that's where the heart of the character is.

BECKY. The heart of Tzeitel is in her nudity?

RABBI SCHWARTZBAUM. It's not in her pajamas. Nudity is the key to her development. We don't need to see the nudity of Chava. Chava nude? It's gratuitous. If Demi Moore played Chava, there'd be a point there, but Tzeitel, yes. Yes; in her perfectly exposed soft body lies her truth.

BECKY. I think I see what you mean, Rabbi. I think I'm catching on. I see the character right before my eyes the more you speak of her. She becomes whole.

RABBI SCHWARTZBAUM. That's because I'm a qualified theatrical director. Oh, this is going to be a fantastic career move for you, Becky.

BECKY. I want to be a dental assistant.

RABBI SCHWARTZBAUM. Then this is going to be a fantastic career move for me, Becky. I chose you for the role of Tsital because you are… you are… beautiful.

BECKY. .I am?

RABBI SCHWARTZBAUM. You have range!

BECKY. I do?

RABBI SCHWARTZBAUM. Guts. I picked you for your guts.

BECKY. I have beauty, range, and guts?

RABBI SCHWARTZBAUM
Guts of William Shakespeare. Or Madonna. You have guts all over the place.

BECKY. I hope I'm not making a mess on your floor all over the place.

(SCHWARTZBAUM moves BECKY, stage left)

RABBI SCHWARTZBAUM. Stand here. Think Tsital. Go on. Tsital.

(SHE makes a weird face)

RABBI SCHWARTZBAUM. What is that?

BECKY. Tsital thinking.

RABBI SCHWARTZBAUM. What is she thinking about? She has cramps?

BECKY. Becoming a dental assistant in the New World.

RABBI SCHWARTZBAUM. Let me help you there, Becky. The most important thing about discovering a character is not thinking. Try Tsital not thinking.

BECKY. I won't think.

RABBI SCHWARTZBAUM. That's a good idea. Try the walk.

BECKY. The walk?

RABBI SCHWARTZBAUM. How a character walks. Very important. Try a Tsital walk.

(BECKY walks with a limp)

RABBI SCHWARTZBAUM. Did Tsital twist an ankle?

BECKY. I thought they were so poor and downtrodden that she might drag a leg.

RABBI SCHWARTZBAUM. Interesting choice. It looks like Tsital was in a skiing accident. Let's try not thinking and not walking.

BECKY. Got it. Tsital not thinking and not walking. I'm learning so much from you, Rabbi Schwartzbaum.

The Bitter Herbs

(THEY smile at each other. Then again, break)

RABBI SCHWARTZBAUM. Let's move on. Let's try seeing how much Tsital loves Motel-The-Tailor.

BECKY. Love?

RABBI SCHWARTZBAUM. Can you love, Becky?

BECKY. Yes, Rabbi. I can love.

RABBI SCHWARTZBAUM. Then... love. For me? For the role of Tsital I mean.

(BECKY throws HER head back, lifts HER skirt, and kicks a leg into the air and puts hand on HER hip)

RABBI SCHWARTZBAUM. This is Tsital having a seizure, no?

BECKY. Tsital in love.

RABBI SCHWARTZBAUM. I want to see Becky in love.

BECKY. Becky in love?

RABBI SCHWARTZBAUM. Seeing Becky in love is seeing Tsital in love.

BECKY. Got it.

(SHE gives a dead-on "in love" glance at the RABBI)

RABBI SCHWARTZBAUM. *(Totally taken by HER)* Oh my. That is good... that is love. Becky in love. Rabbi in love.

BECKY. What is that, rabbi?

RABBI SCHWARTZBAUM. Nothing. Nothing at all. Tsital loves like Becky. Perfect.

BECKY. Yes. Tsital loves like Becky. What next, Rabbi Schwartzbaum?

RABBI SCHWARTZBAUM. Next?

BECKY. What do I do now to express Tsital?

RABBI SCHWARTZBAUM. *(Nervously)* Nothing.

BECKY. If Tsital walks like Becky. And Tsital loves like Becky. That means Tsital's nudity is like Becky's. I should get nude.

(SHE unbuttons HER blouse)

RABBI SCHWARTZBAUM. *Oye gevalt*, what the hell are you doing? Cover yourself up there! I'm a rabbi!

BECKY. You're a director!

RABBI SCHWARTZBAUM. Would you please call and tell my agent that?

BECKY. But you insisted on the nudity.

RABBI SCHWARTZBAUM. I'm calling your parents.

BECKY. Why? Do you wanna hurt them?

RABBI SCHWARTZBAUM. They should know what's going on. What's happening here. In the event they proceed with my ex-communication.

BECKY. You can't call my parents. It will hurt my career.

RABBI SCHWARTZBAUM. Your career as a dental assistant?

BECKY. My career as a qualified professional actress. I like the idea of being an actress now. And stop treating me like a kid, Rabbi. I've been through two years of college. I've lived on my own...briefly...and if this is what takes to be directed by you, Rabbi Schwartzbaum, then this is what it takes.

(SHE unhooks HER skirt. HIS eyes are glued on HER)

RABBI SCHWARTZBAUM. You give one *hellevan* audition, Becky Mizrahi.

The Bitter Herbs

(THEIR eyes meet once again. This time neither can break the mood)

RABBI SCHWARTZBAUM. May I level with you, Becky? Oh, *dahling,* the theater is a dying game.

BECKY. But you can save it, Rabbi Schwartzbaum.

RABBI SCHWARTZBAUM. It's hard to bring audiences in. Impossible even. A theatrical producer must do publicity, mailings, press, you have to sell theater subscriptions, there's no end to the work in getting people into the seats. You understand what I'm trying to tell you, dear?

BECKY. Are you closing down this production, Rabbi? Because that would be totally unfair to me. I have done an enormous amount of character work. Look.

(SHE turns in an odd position)

RABBI SCHWARTZBAUM. Tsital with osteoporosis.

BECKY. Bowling. I thought she'd need a hobby.

RABBI SCHWARTZBAUM. Again. Another way to go.

BECKY. I'm putting my heart and soul into this part. I'm going to be a star. I'm not going to spend the rest of my days poking around gums. This is the start of something special for me. And if my parents see that I can do this. That I can hold an entire production together and sing my heart out as Tsital -- they won't make me go to dental school anymore. I can drop out. Give up my education. Spend more time around the temple. With you. And someday be a great actress -- like Britney Spears.

RABBI SCHWARTZBAUM. You are beautiful, Becky Mizrahi when you talk show biz.

BECKY. Am I?

RABBI SCHWARTZBAUM. *(Tries to stay professional)* What I really want is to get people to the synagogue. Do you know that tomorrow night at Temple

Beth Shalom on East 45th Street, they're doing a full scale all out production of "Equus" starring David Hasselhoff?

BECKY. Is David Hasselhoff Jewish?

RABBI SCHWARTZBAUM. Is Steven Seagal? Is he? And uptown? Temple Torah Emmet? West 92nd. Two months straight they've been running "Nunsense" starring Flava Flav. I'm telling you, Becky, we have to keep up. Or my an entire career is kaput!

BECKY. You mean your career as a qualified theatrical director?

RABBI SCHWARTZBAUM. My career as a rabbi! You've heard of keeping up with the Jones'? I'm keeping up with the Schwartzbaum's. My father. My uncle. My brothers. All rabbis. Every last one of them. Except for my cousin Al -- who's a cantor. Do you know how one judges a successful congregation in New York City these days, Becky?

BECKY. Parking?

RABBI SCHWARTZBAUM. Crowds. Crowds on Rosh Hashana. Crowds on Yom Kippur. Big crowds on Yom Kippur. But most important, crowds on the Sabbath.

BECKY. Sabbath.

RABBI SCHWARTZBAUM. The Saturday crowd. Jews are Jews when it comes to the High Holidays. But have you ever bumped into your average American Jew and he's frantic because he forgot it was Saturday? But if we start putting on good shows. More shows... then... then I can see people getting in touch with their faith and fill our temple every Saturday.

BECKY. Why don't you just have a cake sale?

RABBI SCHWARTZBAUM. Jews don't buy cakes. Unless… it comes with a nice cup of coffee.

BECKY. I can't believe how much about the entertainment industry I'm learning from you. I want to do justice to the role of Tsital in "Fiddler On The

Roof." *(SHE pulls HER top off revealing a sexy bra)* I'm doing this for God.

RABBI SCHWARTZBAUM. He -- could -- see -- you!

BECKY. But this is Tsital's underwear.

(SHE drops HER skirt revealing matching slip)

RABBI SCHWARTZBAUM. *Oye.* (Nervously sits) Can I get you something to drink, Miss Mizrahi?

BECKY. But I'm ready to rehearse the nude scene, Rabbi. Are you nervous?

RABBI SCHWARTZBAUM. You might be surprised to hear this, Miss Mizrahi, but rabbi's have feelings too.

BECKY *(Uncontrollable laughter)* No they don't!

RABBI SCHWARTZBAUM. And emotions.

BECKY. You're being silly now.

RABBI SCHWARTZBAUM. Sit, please. *(SHE does)* When you came in to audition for Tsital, I... *(Pours HIMself a drinks; gulps it down)* ... I immediately saw talent. And something else. *(Another drink)* I saw a very pretty young woman.

(SHE realizes SHE is in HER underwear and becomes self-conscious. SHE grabs two yalmukas and covers HER breasts)

RABBI SCHWARTZBAUM. I'm not trying to scare you.

BECKY. You're a rabbi and you're coming on to me.

RABBI SCHWARTZBAUM. No. No, you've misconstrued this entire thing. I'm a man and I'm coming on to you. I've never been married. And I date very infrequently.

BECKY. Me too.

RABBI SCHWARTZBAUM. When you came to the audition, I thought you were stunning. As hot as Delilah.

BECKY. Was she the blonde tramp who auditioned before me?

RABBI SCHWARTZBAUM. She's from the bible. Samson and Delilah. One pictures her as the pinnacle of beauty.

BECKY. *(Smitten)* I'm the pinnacle of beauty?

RABBI SCHWARTZBAUM. Higher than the pinnacle of beauty. Mountaintop of beauty. Stratosphere of beauty! You're beauty cubed, Becky Mizrahi.

BECKY. OH, Rabbi Schwartzbaum...

RABBI SCHWARTZBAUM. Call me Yonkle.

BECKY. Why?

RABBI SCHWARTZBAUM. That's my name. Yonkle Schwartzbaum.

BECKY. You never think a rabbi would have a first name.

RABBI SCHWARTZBAUM. We have first names. And we have last names. And we have needs and wants.

BECKY. What do you want, Yonkle?

RABBI SCHWARTZBAUM. I want to be more than friends. I want to formally ask you out on a date, Becky Mizrahi. With your parent's permission of course.

BECKY. You really do wanna knife it to them, don't ya? They'll flip if they hear I came in to audition for a play and you got me in my underwear and now you want to date me.

RABBI SCHWARTZBAUM. Good point. But when one has a feeling. When one has an inner emotion that cannot be halted, one must act upon it. God has given us these feelings.

The Bitter Herbs

BECKY. How long have you felt this way?

RABBI SCHWARTZBAUM. Since the very first scene you read for me. It made me weep. Your sheer openness. This is the way it should be, Becky. Love I mean. Two people completely open to each other's lust.

(SHE rises, only in HER underwear, SHE crawls to HIM seductively)

RABBI SCHWARTZBAUM. My guess is we're not going to be staging the Sabbath . Prayer scene now.

BECKY. When I would listen to you *doven*, I would picture myself in your arms.

RABBI SCHWARTZBAUM. That's incredible! I didn't think anyone was listening.

BECKY. Us spinning on a dance floor.

RABBI SCHWARTZBAUM. Or me taking you to see a Broadway musical?

BECKY. A simple dental assistant and a man who looks so sharp in black.

(SHE takes HIS face)

RABBI SCHWARTZBAUM. The only other person to say that to me is the Moil's wife -- and she has clammy hands.

BECKY. I always wanted to kiss you. Do you know what I mean?

RABBI SCHWARTZBAUM. I have no idea what you mean.

BECKY. I'm afraid I'm going to have insist upon the kissing.

(THEY have a tender kiss)

BECKY. I always thought you handsome.

RABBI SCHWARTZBAUM. I always saw you as a star. Come. I'm taking you to the theater.

BECKY. *(Excited)* On a date?

(HE nods. SHE hops off HIM and dresses)

RABBI SCHWARTZBAUM. We'll see them all. "Rent," "Oklahoma," and that one with the strippers: "Man of LaMancha."

BECKY. "Gypsy."

RABBI SCHWARTZBAUM. There are strippers in Gypsy?" I have to call my mother. I have to tell her I found my Tsital.

BECKY. You have parents?

RABBI SCHWARTZBAUM. Rabbi's have parents. Rabbi's have mothers. BOY do rabbi's have mothers! I found my muse! My future.

BECKY. *(Insecure)* Then the part is mine, Yonkle?

RABBI SCHWARTZBAUM. The part is yours, Becky.

(THEY kiss again)

BECKY. I'll make you proud. I promise. And don't you worry, I'm going to deliver for you the best nude scene Sinai Temple of The East Side has ever seen! Complete nudity!

RABBI SCHWARTZBAUM. Are you *meshuga*? You think I'm gonna let my girlfriend show *boobies* to some fish eating dinner theater crowd? I'm a qualified theatrical director!

BECKY. I won't be doing the nudity?

RABBI SCHWARTZBAUM. We save the nudity for Broadway!

(HE puts an arm around HER and THEY exit. BLACKOUT.)

THE PLOT

The living room of EFFIE, 30's, sparsely decorated and a bit of a mess. A sofa, two chairs, the usual.

The doorbell rings and EFFIE shuffles in from HER bedroom, depressed and tired. SHE has dark hair, deep features, and in stained bathrobe with HER hair held up with a butterfly pin. SHE opens the door and like a grandam, HER mother, DESDEMONA, enters in Bergdorf Goodman dress, large-framed dark sunglasses, leather gloves, and a stylish scarf.

DESDEMONA. Darling, I am going to say this once and only once. You are never to make mention of it again. If I hear you make mention of it again, I am going to deny it, reject it and pretend you have lost all senses of reality and I will disown you as your mother. (*Sits, folds HER hand over her lap*) Don't you offer a guest coffee or a piece of danish when they come to your home?

EFFIE. If a guest came to my... Okay, Mother.

DESDEMONA. Attitude. That's what you're famous for, my dear. But you are not going to give me attitude about this. This is something very serious.

EFFIE. (*Worried*) Is it Dad?

DESDEMONA. I said serious -- not irritating.

EFFIE. Fine, Mother. (*EFFIE exits*)

DESDEMONA. I'm telling you that father of yours...when I think about him. I could have been the Duchess of Kent. Instead, I married the Duke of Flatbush! The man is like a child. I treat him like a child. The other day he came in from the yard and his feet were covered in dirt. I sent him right to his room and for a shower. Oh he pouted and all, but I had to lay the law down. Do you have any idea what that new two-tone shag carpeting cost?

(*EFFIE enters with a cup of coffee and a danish*)

EFFIE. Are you going to tell me?

DESDEMONA. (*Without a beat*) Twenty-five dollars a square foot!

EFFIE. A foot.

DESDEMONA. Twenty-five dollars a square foot. Yes! Cost me a fortune. Anyway, that father of yours treats that carpet like it was a door mat. I tell you this -- a doormat does not cost twenty-five dollars a square foot. What's this?

EFFIE. Coffee and a danish.

DESDEMONA. What am I supposed to do with it?

EFFIE. Mother. You said a good host would offer coffee and a danish.

DESDEMONA. Yes. But a good guest always says, "No thank you, don't bother on my account." Why didn't you ask?

EFFIE. Because I -- Never mind. (*EFFIE shakes HER head and exits*)

DESDEMONA. Darling, I am going to say this once and only once. Can you hear me in there?

EFFIE. (*Off-Stage*) Even if I try not to.

DESDEMONA. You are never to make mention of it again. If I hear you make mention of it again, I am going to deny it, reject it and pretend you were institutionalized for reasons only your doctor knows for sure. Do you want me to tell you this?

(*EFFIE enters*)

EFFIE. Are you going to tell me this?

The Bitter Herbs

DESDEMONA. Caustic.

(EFFIE mouths the word "Caustic")

DESDEMONA. -- That's what you're famous for. But you're not going to be caustic about this. This is something very important. *(EFFIE sits, looks at her mother)*

EFFIE. So... what's the big issue?

DESDEMONA. Don't you offer a guest a pillow for their back?

EFFIE. If I had a guest... Okay, Mother. *(EFFIE reluctantly exits)*

DESDEMONA. Your father isn't much of a host either, I'll tell you that, Effie. We once had a cocktail party for some of his business associates... or as I like to call them... "The boys from the shop who can't read or write." Anyway, that man, your father, didn't buy enough wine. There wasn't enough bread. The fish was cold. Cold fish. And halfway through he decided to do his imitation of Sammy Davis Jr. It was tasteless. Where he got the idea that covering his face with chocolate pudding would make the imitation more realistic, he makes me sick. The man makes me sick.

(EFFIE enters with a pillow poised to suffocate HER mouth)

EFFIE. M-M-M-M--mother?

DESDEMONA. *(Turns to HER)* Yes, dear?

EFFIE. *(Gently)* Might I offer you a pillow for your back?

DESDEMONA. Am I some old lady? My back is fine. Now if you had something for the arthritis in my knee, then you'd be some daughter.

(EFFIE falls back on to the sofa and tries to suffocate HERself with the pillow)

EFFIE. So, no pillow.

DESDEMONA. No pillow.

EFFIE. No pillow.

DESDEMONA. Aren't you going to offer your guest --

EFFIE. --No --

DESDEMONA. -- Very well, darling. Then let's just get to it. I am going to say this once and only once. Do you promise never to bring it up again?

EFFIE. (*A la Groucho*) Especially if I never hear it.

DESDEMONA. Your father and I went up to Mount Shalom in Medford. Exit Seventy-Four on the Long Island Expressway. If it was any further, the people there would be speaking Chinese. And don't get me started on what two hours in the car alone with your father is like.

EFFIE. What were you doing at the cemetery, Mother?

DESDEMONA. I was getting a tan -- what do you think I was doing at the cemetery? Okay, I'll say it. Your father and I bought plots.

EFFIE. I see. Well... you're both okay, right?

DESDEMONA. I'm fine, perfectly fine. If you're judging your father, physically he has the constitution of a zebra and can eat crap like others eat caviar. His mental state is another thing... yesterday I caught him drinking two bottles of Red Wine. He said something about not wanting to hear me complain about how he never puts the dishes in the dish washer correctly, but I know it's because his boss cut down his hours and it's upsetting him. Like we really need men on the factory line getting more cocoa puffs to the market. Your father thinks he's curing Cancer. All he really does is give young children bad teeth.

EFFIE. Well you're both doing fine. (*Drinks the coffee SHE brought for HER mother*) I guess getting plots is the smart thing to do. It's very responsible of both of you.

DESDEMONA. Not for us, Effie, the plots are for you.

EFFIE. (*Spits the coffee out*) For me?

DESDEMONA. You think your father is going to die? That man is going to live forever. Him and his drunken buddies who barely speak or write English. But boy can they shove a small little plastic whistle into a box of cereal with class.

EFFIE. You bought me a cemetery plot?

DESDEMONA. We got a fabulous deal. If you die before you're eighty -- we get free gardening for ten years.

EFFIE. That's terrible.

DESDEMONA. No. It cost a lot of money to keep up the grass and flowers in a place like Mount Shalom in Medford. I think it's worth it.

EFFIE. I'm not dying before I'm eighty!

DESDEMONA. Of course you're not, Effie. I'm just saying, if you did... we took the extra step of making sure you're not just sitting in dirt. You'll have tulips.

EFFIE. I don't like tulips.

DESDEMONA. I love tulips.

EFFIE. Why did you feel you needed to get me a funeral plot?

DESDEMONA. Because you're too irresponsible to do it yourself. Short sighted -- that's what you're famous for.

EFFIE. (*Losing patience*) I'm thirty-two! Are you going to live my life for me?!

DESDEMONA. -- You'll thank me for this, Effie. When you're lying there face up in the ground at Mount Shalom in Medford, in my favorite pink and green Oscar de la Renta gown, which is not as stained as that bathrobe you're always traipsing around in -- you will thank me -- and I will be on your mind.

EFFIE. That's my biggest nightmare.

DESDEMONA. It's never too early to think about the grim reaper, Effie. You were always like this. You didn't want to get your period either -- but I told you it would happen. And sure enough...

EFFIE. -- Yes, well you told me when I was five!

DESDEMONA. The point is... death comes to everyone and your father and I thought we would do this nice thing for you. Hey -- you promised never to make mention of it again.

EFFIE. I've only just begun to mention it. No, Mother. This is serious.

DESDEMONA. But if I hear you make mention of it again, I am going to deny it, reject it and pretend you have deep seeded psychological problems from your father's brother Benjamin who to this day thinks he's the world famous athlete... Sea Biscuit.

EFFIE. I don't like the way this feels, Mother. The thought that there's a place for me... up there.

DESDEMONA. It's Medford. You love the Island.

EFFIE. Yes. For the food.

DESDEMONA. You'll be near Jack.

EFFIE. Jack?

DESDEMONA. Jackie. *(Gets emotional)* My adopted Greyhound I saved from the prison of South Florida where they raced her around the track chasing a rabbit like she was some animal.

EFFIE. Jackie Onassis was a dog.

DESDEMONA. Don't you talk that way about the president's wife!

EFFIE. I'm talking about the dog!

DESDEMONA. Well. If my little standard white poodle John was seen as my little president, I guess that does make my beloved Greyhound Jackie -- First-Dog.

EFFIE. This is not my life! This is a terrible life! I am not going to take this from you anymore, Mother. I hate you! You hear me? I HATE YOU! And I am not going to be buried in some plot at Mount Shalom in Medford in your stinking favorite pink and green Oscar de la Renta gown just so you can control me from the grave -- it's not going to happen, it's not in the cards, you evil, manipulative, dominating, power-hungry old woman!!! I am worth more than that... I am more important than that -- I demand a better life!!!

(EFFIE is about to cry as SHE crosses to the front door and opens it)

DESDEMONA. *(Long pause)* How can anyone speak of an Oscar de la Renta gown with such disdain? I've never been so disappointed in my own daughter, Effie.

EFFIE. *(Slow turn)* Have you heard a single word I just --

DESDEMONA. -- Anyway Jackie is buried just across the way from your plots. But if you peek between some trees, you can see her headstone. I got you matching ones. Jackie's has a picture of a little pooch on it. Yours I'm thinking will be a granite likeness of you in that stained bathrobe.

EFFIE. I'm near the pet cemetery?

DESDEMONA. Well it was either that or the view of the Long Island Expressway, and let's be honest, dear, you have such road rage.

EFFIE. Alright, fine. Let's not talk about this anymore.

DESDEMONA. I was asking for that.

(After a moment of silence)

EFFIE. Can I get you some lunch?

DESDEMONA. Dear, you don't offer a guest lunch with your abilities in the kitchen. Are you trying to kill your own mother?

EFFIE. You are impossible!

DESDEMONA. I'm just being nice. And honest.

EFFIE. You're always correcting me, telling me what to do, how to do it. Never a pat on the back. Thirty-two and I feel I have never done anything to live up to your high standards. Maybe I should just kill you -- this way you'll get out of my hair and be up at Mount Shalom in Medford.

DESDEMONA. *(Laughs)* Oh I'm not being buried up in that hell hole, Effie.

EFFIE. You're not?

DESDEMONA. Your father and I like the city life. We have a mausoleum up on East 86th. Overlooking the park.

EFFIE. You're overlooking the park and I'm overlooking dogs and feline distemper victims?

DESDEMONA. Well you won't be alone.

EFFIE. I'm having company? But I'm a terrible host.

DESDEMONA. Effie. I'm going to say this once and only once. You should consider therapy.

EFFIE. Me? You! You should consider therapy.

DESDEMONA. First the pink gown, now this. It's a call for help, Effie. A call. Now your father and I have taken the necessary steps to secure buying you two plots.

EFFIE. Two plots?

DESDEMONA. For your husband. And you.

EFFIE. I'm not married.

DESDEMONA. You will.

EFFIE. I'm not dating.

DESDEMONA. You will.

EFFIE. I'm a lesbian.

DESDEMONA. They have cures.

EFFIE. I am not going through this with you again.

DESDEMONA. That's what I was asking for!

EFFIE. I cannot believe you would do this to me. Behind my back! You bought a plot for a person I haven't met yet!?

DESDEMONA. A MAN. A man you haven't met yet. Yes. This is just like the time I told you those breasts of yours would grow just like your grandmother's -- she has to carry them around in a supermarket basket -- and I insisted we buy you a training bra.

EFFIE. When I was seven.

DESDEMONA. The point is I have always been prepared and I want you to be prepared for this.

EFFIE. For meeting a man I can be buried with.

DESDEMONA. Yes.

EFFIE. Even though I like girls.

DESDEMONA. I think you understand now. I might have just saved you money on your first therapy session.

EFFIE. So I'm supposed to tell a guy I just met that I already have a cemetery plot for him across the street from my mother's rescued Greyhound?

DESDEMONA. Well don't bring it up on the first date of course, Effie, you wait. Maybe on your second date, you can pack a picnic basket and head out to Medford for a day in the sun.

EFFIE. -- And nonchalantly spread out fried chicken and corn on the cob across the plots we're going to be buried in.

DESDEMONA. I thought we weren't going to talk about this?

EFFIE. You weren't going to talk about this, Mother, but I am going to talk about this. You crossed a line with this. You've been pushing your way into my life for years, but you've gone too far this time.

DESDEMONA. By doing such a nice thing?

EFFIE. By controlling!

DESDEMONA. You call it controlling. I call it love.

EFFIE. You won't even accept the fact that I'm gay.

DESDEMONA. I do accept the fact that you're gay. I also accept the fact that someday you'll be gay with a man.

EFFIE. I'm never going to get through to you!

DESDEMONA. Imagine how I feel?

EFFIE. I give up.

DESDEMONA. I'm not saying another word.

EFFIE. Good!

(EFFIE sits. Both women unable to communicate. Silence. Then...)

DESDEMONA. I don't think they allow two women to be buried in the same marital plot, Effie.

EFFIE. I probably won't ever meet anyone anyway. Look at me. I'm a mess.

DESDEMONA. You're not. You're just different. I always told your father you were different. You were like him. You were both very different. Oh my God -- your father's a lesbian.

EFFIE. (*Laughs*) I don't think so.

DESDEMONA. Eccentric. I call him eccentric. Especially when I'm not talking to him. I can call you eccentric if you'd like.

EFFIE. I hate my job. I can't meet anyone. I have a stained bathrobe. What's wrong with me, Mother?

DESDEMONA. Nothing that can't be turned around, Effie. You'll see. You'll turn this all around.

(*More silence*)

EFFIE. You want to buy me something in the future, don't buy me a plot -- buy me a blouse.

DESDEMONA. You know I can't do that, Effie. You have such terrible taste, how am I ever going to buy you something you like? (*Touches the robe*) This won't come clean anymore, will it?

EFFIE. You talk about my attitude... what about your attitude? I'm the way I am because you're the way you are.

DESDEMONA. (*SHE has no comeback*) I guess you are.

(*THEY sit but can't look at each other. Long pause*)

DESDEMONA. I might have just saved you money on your second therapy session. So. Now that you know what's wrong with you, you can help yourself.

EFFIE. I just have to realize I shouldn't be like you in any way shape or form and I'll be fine.

DESDEMONA. Exactly.

(SHE realizes what SHE just said and cannot face EFFIE)

EFFIE. Before I die, Mother... I would want us to be friends.

DESDEMONA. (*Softens*) We're already friends, Effie. (*Off a look from EFFIE*) Okay, we can be better friends.

EFFIE. Thank you.

(They both nod)

EFFIE. And I want you to be nicer to dad.

DESDEMONA. You just want to hurt me, don't you? (*Off another look*) Alright. Fine. I'll be nicer to the *putz.*

EFFIE. Thank you.

DESDEMONA. So... Is sex with dykes fulfilling?

EFFIE. You should probably leave now.

DESDEMONA. Good idea.

(DESDEMONA puts on HER scarf and gloves)

EFFIE. Thanks for coming by, Mother.

DESDEMONA. The plots are there if you want them, Effie. If you don't want them, maybe your children or... lesbians have children, don't they, Effie?

EFFIE. Good-bye, Mother.

(DESDEMONA puts on HER sunglasses and cross to the door)

DESDEMONA. Darling, I am going to say this once and only once. You are never to make mention of it again. If I hear you make mention of it again, I am going to deny it, reject it and pretend I am not your mother.

EFFIE. (*With a smile*) Don't tempt me -- just say it.

DESDEMONA. I'm proud you're my daughter. *(EFFIE is blown away)* Yes. So you hate your job. Get a new job. You're smart enough. You can be anything you want to be. So you can't meet anyone. Go on-line. You never know... there's a lot of pretty girls on line, Effie. I see your lazy crack-pot father looking at them all the time. But... I'm nice to him. *(EFFIE smiles)* And as for that stained bathrobe. Well... it looks good on you.

(SHE turns to go, then back)

DESDEMONA. Don't you offer a guest a kiss when they leave?

(EFFIE crosses to HER and kisses HER mom's cheek)

DESDEMONA. You're a good hostess, Effie. Someday you're going to make someone a fabulous eccentric... husband?

(SHE tosses the scarf over HER shoulder and exits. EFFIE thinks for a beat, then dials the phone)

EFFIE. (Into phone) Donna? It's Effie. From the gym. I'm in your spin class? (*Beat*) Monday's Tuesday's Wednesday's Thursday's and Friday's. (*Beat*) So, uhm, I was thinking... I mean, I'm not even sure you're a... lez... Maybe you and I can go out for a drink after a workout some time. You know. A drink, a smoke, it'll be good for us. Get the endorphins going. (*Realizes SHE'S striking out*) Maybe on our second date, I can pack a picnic basket and head out to Medford -- I already have a cemetery plot for us across the street from my mother's rescued Greyhound. (*No beat*) Okay, Donna. I'll find a new spin class tomorrow.

(SHE hangs up... waves HER arms madly at HER mother. Gathers HERself... dials again)

EFFIE. Lisa? It's Effie... From pilates...

(Slow fade to BLACKOUT)

HOOD RATZ

Set: A living room in an apartment in the Fairfax District of Los Angeles. Sofa center, chair and table. Door, upstage, right.

It's Early Morning. BEN KATZ, 30s, stands center, dressed in corporate button down short sleeve shirt, dark slacks, and leather shoes. HE attempts to put on Tefillin *(phylacteries). BEN is not great at it. HE looks more like a mummy with the leather straps hanging loose and awkward. HE grows frustrated but hides it well.*

ARTHUR. (*Off-Stage*)You think we're much alike, Ben? (*Beat*) You think we're alike? Similar?

(ARTHUR, HIS brother, enters, also *awkwardly bound in the teffillin leather straps hanging loosely off HIS arm and head. HE is dressed identical.*

ARTHUR. I feel like I've been attacked by giant licorice.

BEN. Brothers are brothers. Similar is similar. Same beliefs, same problems, same dreams, same same. Ready? (*Prays*) *Baruch ata Adonai elohanynu melech ha'olam asher kidshanu bemitzvotav vetzivanu lehani'ach tefillin.* They say when you grow up with someone, you take on the habits of the other person. Nature vs Nurture. Ready? (*Prays*) *Baruch ata Adonai elohanynu melech ha'olam asher kidshanu bemitzvotav vetzivanu al mitzvat tefillin.*

ARTHUR. Hey. It's like "Snakes on A Plane."

BEN. We can't forget that the two of us grew up for most of our lives without a mother and father. Think about it, Arthur. If you had grown up with a gorilla, you would take on the habits of such gorilla.

ARTHUR. I don't want to be a gorilla, Ben.

BEN. None of us do. (*Prays*) *Baruch shem kvod malchuso leolam vaed.*

ARTHUR/BEN. Amen.

BEN. -- There's nothing to worry about, Arthur. I've taken care of you since Momma and Poppa went to heaven, and I will continue to take care of you no matter what. Now take off your *teffilin*, we'll have some breakfast. I made your favorite.

ARTHUR. *Blintzes*?

BEN. Toast. Then we'll go to work. I packed a lunch. Your favorite.

ARTHUR. Peanut butter and jelly?

BEN. Roast chicken and mustard.

ARTHUR. (*As HE packs the teffilin*) I never did get used to putting these things on.

BEN. You see. We're practically twins in this respect. So we do it.

ARTHUR. We do it wrong.

BEN. All the time. But we try. Always trying. And if he, *hashem*, wills it, we will keep trying.

ARTHUR. And soon there will be three of us. Right, Ben? Three of us.

BEN. Arthur, if God is on our side, if he, *hashem,* wills it, then we will be a united family. For the first time. Just think of it. After all these years, a brother.

ARTHUR. A new brother.

BEN. Huh? Yes! So when the private detective calls --

ARTHUR. She called, Ben. The private detective.

BEN. She called? Why didn't you tell me she called? Arthur! What did she say?

ARTHUR. She said she's coming right over. To give us news.

BEN. Clean up, Arthur... this could be it. This could be the news we've been praying for.

(As THEY tidy up, the doorbell rings.)

BEN. Get the door. I'll put out some treats... Your favorite...

ARTHUR. Cotton candy?

BEN. Chocolates. Go, go, go.

(BEN puts a box of chocolates on the table as ARTHUR opens the door and SALLY PEABODY enters. SHE wears a black trench coat, and large fedora. SHE is slightly Sam Spade so far as to enter the room and shadow the wall as if being followed. SHE speaks with a thick Russian accent.)

ARTHUR. Miss Peabody.

SALLY. Anybody else here?

ARTHUR points to BEN.

BEN. I have a chicken in the kitchen. I was making lunch.

SALLY. When you hired me, I had no idea the journey I was going to undertake. The places I would see, and the people I would meet. I traveled to New York, and London. Spain and Madrid. (*SHE looks around to make sure nobody caught her lie*) I backpacked, and rode motor scooters. Logged frequent flyer miles and learned to pull a rickshaw. And finally I have the most amazing news.

ARTHUR. You found our brother.

SALLY. (*SHE speaks without the accent...it was a fake*) Why'd you ruin it for me? I wanted to be the one to tell you. (*Frustrated; puts on accent*) All right. All right. Through exhaustive means... your parent's identification, DNA testing, and cross-checking facts and figures... I have found the boy that your momma and poppa gave up when they were young teenagers.

ARTHUR. I could cry.

BEN. Stay strong, Arthur. The Katz men stay strong.

ARTHUR. Tell us more, Miss Peabody. Does he look like us?

SALLY. The resemblance is striking.

BEN. Imagine that. Imagine that, Arthur.

SALLY. -- And you won't in a million years guess where your long lost brother actually lives.

ARTHUR. Right in this neighborhood.

SALLY. (*The accent is gone*) Why'd you ruin it for me? I wanted to be the one to tell you.

BEN. Arthur, stop ruining it for her. He lives around here.

ARTHUR. It's like mother and father are back with us.

BEN. It's a miracle. It's the miracle of Passover.

ARTHUR. It is?

BEN. Yes of course. The Jewish people -- exiled from the Land of Goshen after the plagues were brought down upon Egypt. We have been plagued, Arthur. A shroud has always been over us wondering if our older brother was safe. Happy. And if he carried on the traditions of our family. (*To SALLY*) Miss Peabody, have you met him? Have you met our brother yet?

SALLY. I have. We had dinner last night.

BEN. Dinner?

SALLY. Last night. It was very romantic.

BEN. It was? Why?

ARTHUR. -- So he eats. (*THEY look at HIM*) Oh I knew my brother would eat. I love him already.

BEN. Might I ask -- Was it a Kosher meal, Miss Peabody?

SALLY. Your brother is Glatt Kosher, Ben. The biggest Kosher anyone can be. And he's a big tipper. And hands, very soft.

BEN. Excuse me...?

ARTHUR. He's Kosher, Ben. Our brother is Kosher. Miss Peabody, what did my brother eat?

SALLY. Blintzes.

BEN. Oh my Lord, Arthur... did you hear that?

ARTHUR. Blintzes are my favorite food. Next to *kishka*, potato *latke,* and Popeye's Fried Chicken.

BEN. (*To HER*) What did he say at dinner, Miss Peabody? What are his intentions?

SALLY. Oh we talked about many things. All night long in fact. He has a beautiful baritone voice.

BEN. What? No, no... Did he speak about his childhood?

ARTHUR. He had a childhood, didn't he?

SALLY. Your brother had a childhood, Arthur.

ARTHUR. So he was a child! I knew it! I knew my brother would have been a child.

SALLY. He spoke kindly of his adoptive parents.

BEN. And they were of the Jewish persuasion?

SALLY. Freakin' big Jews.

ARTHUR. He's a Jew!

BEN. (*Arms raised high*)YES!

(*ARTHUR and BEN dance around the sofa like an impromptu "Hava Nagila."*)

BEN. Miss Peabody. May I ask? Did he attend Yeshiva?

SALLY. He did, Ben. As a young man.

BEN. Arthur! Our brother was a Yeshiva student.

ARTHUR. A Yeshiva student who was a child and who eats. Holy Cow!

(*One more dance around the sofa.*)

BEN. It's another miracle. The miracle of Hanukkah.

ARTHUR. It is?

BEN. Yes of course. The Jewish people only had enough oil to make the menorah light for one night. But it lasted eight nights. We thought it was just the two of us, Arthur. Two boys without parents left alone to fend for themselves. It turns out there is enough love for three. Three! (*To SALLY*) So you had dinner, then...

SALLY. Then?

BEN. Then what happened?

SALLY. Well obviously we went dancing -- duh.

(*ARTHUR and BEN look at each other.*)

SALLY. Then this morning at his apartment...

BEN. You were at his apartment?

SALLY. This morning.

BEN. This morning?

ARTHUR. Our brother's apartment?

BEN. You spent the night?

SALLY. We had a very nice breakfast together. French toast.

ARTHUR. Oh I hope he's not French, Ben.

BEN. Miss Peabody, are you telling us you had breakfast, after having dinner and spending the night with this man? What is going on, Miss Peabody?

SALLY. (*Resume accent*) You insult me, Mr. Katz. I am a professional, licensed by this state under a grant to an off-shore internet site.

(Normal Voice) I paid them twelve dollars! I was doing my job. Slowly getting to know this hot hot burning ring of fire of a man. And I have come to the conclusion that he would make an excellent husband -- <u>brother</u>. I said brother!

BEN. Miss Peabody -- you are dating our long lost brother!

SALLY. *(Normal voice)* -- I'm going to be paid, right? Paid?

ARTHUR. What's his name?

SALLY. His name?

BEN. Did you get his name while you were eating and dancing and waking up in his apartment for french toast this morning?

SALLY. His name is Yewande.

ARTHUR. His name is Yewande?

BEN. Yehuda?

SALLY. Yewande.

BEN. Yehuda?

SALLY. His name is Yewande.

ARTHUR. It's an interesting name. Do you think Momma named him that, Ben?

BEN. Is it from the Old Testament?

ARTHUR. It sounds old.

SALLY. I have one more surprise.

ARTHUR. He's coming here right now.

SALLY. Okay, you're not making this fun for me at all.

(The doorbell rings. SHE throws up HER arms.)

BEN. Why am I so nervous all of a sudden? The Katz men never get nervous.

ARTHUR. I should put out something to eat. *(HE points)* Chocolate!
 Cuz he eats!

BEN. Our brother. Our Jewish brother. Open the door, Arthur. Go, go, go.

(ARTHUR opens the door, and a tall, muscular, bald, African American man in "wife beater" top and very tight jeans, enters, smiling broadly.)

YEWANDE. My *Mishpucha!*

BEN. Holy shit.

ARTHUR. Hide the silverware!

YEWANDE. It's a *hekaya.*

BEN. And he's an illegal alien who doesn't speak English.

SALLY. Ben and Arthur Katz. I would like you to meet your brother. The very handsome, broad-shouldered, sexier than all hell -- Yewande.

ARTHUR. His name is Yewande?

BEN. Yehuda?

SALLY. Yewande.

BEN. Yehuda?

YEWANDE. Yewande Manatoba.

BEN. Manatoba? That is definitely not from the Old Testament.

ARTHUR. Are you part of the Manatoba family that put in the swimming pool at Torah Et Sh'ma Temple on Pico?

YEWANDE. No. I'm part of the Manatoba family that came from Angola in the underbelly of a slave ship and built up most of Savannah.

ARTHUR. (*To BEN*) I'm sure they're very nice people too.

SALLY. Why don't we sit down, Yewande?

BEN. Yehuda?

SALLY/ARTHUR. Yewande!

(*BEN throws THEM a look.*)

SALLY. Next to me would be fine. We can cuddle and share a glass of cognac. (*To the others*) You <u>do</u> have cognac, don't you?

BEN. What? No!

(*SHE yanks YEWANDE so hard HE goes flying to sit next to HER.*)

SALLY. Here. Sit.

YEWANDE. *Ahsante.* (*To the others*) It means "Thank You."

(*There is cold silence until ARTHUR leans in to BEN.*)

ARTHUR. Say something, Ben, he's scaring me.

BEN. So Sally tells us your name is --

YEWANDE. -- Yewande. It's an African Yoruba name. It means "Mother has returned."

ARTHUR. If she did, she'd drop dead of a heart attack.

BEN. Arthur! (*Beat*) Will you excuse me a moment, please, Yehuda.

YEWANDE. Yewande.

BEN. Arthur!

(*THEY move to stage left, and whisper.*)

BEN. Hide your wallet. He's clearly after our money and our property.

ARTHUR. We don't have any money or property.

BEN. Then he's after our poverty and our depression.

ARTHUR. Could he really be our long lost brother, Ben?

BEN. You see any similarities? Does he talk like Momma?

YEWANDE. *Hey, dog, you got a nice crib here -- really flav... thanks for representing. I could certainly hit skins with some boom around here if I was gangsta, but I ain't into meeting some Jakes.*

ARTHUR. That don't sound like Momma!

(*SALLY joins THEM.*)

SALLY. He's smokin' hot, isn't he? I mean I'm not the only one that sees it, right?

BEN. (*To HER*) The resemblance is striking! What's wrong with you? I did not hire you for this to turn into a J-Date, Miss Peabody... That man is not our brother!

SALLY. Why? Because he doesn't look like you, or talk like you? I resent the fact that you think this whole thing was set up just so that you two would pay me and that all I really wanted was to meet a Black Rock God. Like Seal.

BEN. In order for him to be my brother, Miss Peabody, my mother would have had to... have... my mother would have been involved with a... a Katz woman would never...

(ARTHUR offers chocolates to YEWANDE.)

YEWANDE. *Chakleti! Hawa ya moyo chakleti.* (*Smiles*) That means I have a deep love for chocolate.

ARTHUR. Me too. You should try the dark ones. Once you've had those, you never go back.

SALLY. Look at the three of you. Like a mirror. (*To BEN*) I'm going to be paid, right? Paid? (*Over to YEWANDE*) Dancing again, tonight, right? Salsa? Merengue? Lap?

BEN. Okay... this is not right. We're Jewish. We have been Jewish for a very long time. Like always! We are very Jewish.

YEWANDE. I betcha my people have been Jewish a lot longer than your people have.

BEN. (*To SALLY*) I want proof. You hear me? I want proof that this man is my brother or you don't get a penny from us.

YEWANDE. You want proof?

SALLY. Notice how his muscles tense perfectly when he gets angry. Yumm.

YAWENDE. Did you want proof <u>before</u> you met me?

BEN. Yes, Mr. Manatoba. I want proof. Tell them Arthur. If I say I want proof then I want proof.

ARTHUR. Ben wants proof. (*To YEWANDE*) So if you have to beat the crap out of somebody -- it should be him.

SALLY. I've done my research, Mr. Katz. It seems that right before your parents were married, your mother had a small, insignificant affair.

ARTHUR. (*To YEWANDE*) I don't think it's insignificant. You're at least a hundred and forty pounds.

BEN. Shut up, Arthur! Go on, Miss Peabody.

SALLY. It was a one night affair. Your father knew about it and helped your mother through the process of birth and then adoption. But they stayed together, it made them stronger.

BEN. But how, why... one night? What was so great about this man? This man that almost ruined my life -- who almost kept me from having life -- that now brings this stranger into my world. What was so important about that man?

SALLY. Your mother was very involved in the temple. I hear a lot of people are drawn into relationships with their rabbi.

ARTHUR. Momma *shtuped* the rabbi?

YEWANDE. It's a *hekaya*.

BEN. Again with that?! Look I am not buying any of this. A Black rabbi? What is this San Francisco?

YEWANDE. I'm a rabbi's son. I told you there was lots of us.

BEN. I have to sit down. (*Sits. Stares at YEWANDE*) I have nothing in common with you.

YEWANDE. You have the Torah.

BEN. Totally overrated.

ARTHUR. Ben!

BEN. I don't know what I'm saying.

YEWANDE. We have the Five Books of Moses. We have the *Midrash*. We have the thirteen textual tools attributed to the Tanna Rabbi Ishmael used in the interpretation of Jewish Law *halakha*. Of course we have Rabbi Eliezer's narrative of the more important events of the Pentateuch. And we have the popular but oft mentioned religious celebration of *Shmini Atzeres*.

BEN. I need a Tylenol.

SALLY. We'll take a quick run to CVS for headache pills. Then back for a dual massage. *(To the others)* You <u>do</u> have massage oils, don't you?

BEN. What? No!

YEWANDE. So... What do you boys do for a living?

BEN. We're accountants. What do you do?

YEWANDE. I'm a Certified Public Accountant for the state of California in the legislative branch.

ARTHUR. Wow.(*To BEN*) Is that good?

BEN. I'm talking, Arthur! (*To YEWANDE*) Funny how we all became accountants. Eh, Miss Peabody.

YEWANDE. Tell me more about Momma.

BEN. (*Forced into it*) Momma was a saint. She raised us to be good thinking scholarly men. To ask the right questions when making decisions. To speak with the rabbi. To honor our people, and our traditions.

ARTHUR. She did more than speak with the rabbi.

BEN. Arthur!

ARTHUR. I'm just saying.

YEWANDE. Oh I love the traditions.

SALLY. Isn't he the dreamiest when he talks *shul*? (*THEY all look at HER*) Well he is!

YEWANDE. You know what my favorite tradition is? That if you are born to a Jewish mother... you are automatically Jewish. It's a free pass. True. No other religion in the world can say that. There is no birthright for Roman Catholics. You need to be Baptized. Muslims. Buddhists. You have to study, you have to work at it. Prove yourself. All we have to do is be born. Oh no... I am as much a Jew as the two of you -- believe me, I know that.

BEN. (*With an unpleasant taste*) Yes. We know that too.

YEWANDE. You don't like the fact that I might be your brother, do you, Ben? (*Rises*) Maybe I can put your minds at ease.

SALLY. Yes, yes he can do that. And after, you and I can take a warm bubble bath and loofah each other up. *(To the others)* You do have a loofah, don't you?

BEN. Miss Peabody! Stop this! (*HE circles YEWANDE*) You think you can put my mind at ease, Mr. Manatoba? Put our minds at ease. Tell me how you done good by yourself. Pulled yourself up by your bootstraps. Thought every day and night about what your real mother was like? Eh? Worked your way out of the projects.

SALLY. Yewande grew up in Tarzana.

BEN. Shut up!

ARTHUR. (*Whispers to BEN*) Do they have projects in Tarzana, Ben?

BEN. Would you please stay out of this, Arthur? (*To Yewande*) Make your case. Manatoba. Make it and leave.

YEWANDE. I would have done anything to meet my birth mother. You know why? Because... then I would know why I have this feeling... this feeling deep inside of me, gnawing at my bones... biting at my fingertips. To answer that one question. That one undeniable question that has been with me my entire life! (*Beat*) Why is it I love *matzoh*?

SALLY. He's so cute with the Hebrew.

BEN. Well, it was really unpleasant meeting you...

ARTHUR. But, Ben...

BEN. Arthur. The Katz men are not like this person. (*To YEWANDE*) I am sure, sometime in the future, you are more than welcome to send us a Rosh Hashana card... Get the door, Arthur, go, go, go!

(*ARTHUR doesn't move.*)

SALLY. Mr. Katz... You can't just throw him out...

BEN. If you want payment for this, Miss Peabody, see my lawyer.

ARTHUR.(*Finally standing up to HIS brother*) We can't afford a lawyer, Ben.

(*BEN nods, finally agreeing with his baby brother.*)

SALLY. Keep your money. I was just trying to do the right thing. And make a home. A family. Live in Tujunga and raise a shit-load of Manatoba children.

(*YEWANDE starts to go then stops. ARTHUR moves to shake HIS hand and HE and YEWANDE do a rapper-style shake which confuses ARTHUR to no end. Then THEY hug.*)

YEWANDE. Someday, Ben, someday you are going to think of me. That your mother gave me life. And you are going to want to talk to me. Maybe about your family. Or the Torah. Or maybe just to say Shalom. I hope you will. *(YEWANDE heads for the door when HE sees the teffilin on the table. HE laughs.)* Hmm. Daddy always laughed when I put these on. (HE starts to go.)

ARTHUR. You put on the *teffillin*? Ben?

(THEY watch as YEWANDE puts on the teffilin perfectly. No strings hanging. HE looks great in it.)

YEWANDE. *Baruch ata Adonai elohanynu melech ha'olam asher kidshanu bemitzvotav vetzivanu…*

ARTHUR. *(Tries to say it)* … *vetsss… veso…vano…*

YEWANDE. *(Helps HIM to pronounce)* …*lehani'ach… tefillin.*

YEWANDE/ARTHUR. … *lechani'ach… teffilin.*

ARTHUR. He did it right! Ben! Yewande Manatoba put on the *teffilin* correctly. You can't even do that!

BEN. Yeah well... but...

ARTHUR. Similar is not similar.

BEN. Arthur?

ARTHUR. It's the miracle of... of... a... Martin Luther King Day!

SALLY. It is?

ARTHUR. Momma and Poppa sent Yewande here to teach us. There was no point in them sending another one of us... we need to learn from him. To be good practicing Jews together. To accept all peoples into our lives regardless of creed, or color....

SALLY. (*Re: YEWANDE*) -- Or drop dead gorgeous. I really wish you'd all see the truth in that.

BEN. Poppa always said that one day after he was long gone someone would come into my life and I would know it was meant to be. I was hoping he was talking about Jessica Alba. But no. It's you. You are my brother.

YEWANDE. Well. If he, *hashem,* wills it, it will be.

(*THEY hug. BEN finally smiles.*)

SALLY. (*With great satisfaction*) I did it. I am a professional private investigator. Those were the best twelve dollars I ever spent! (*THEY all look at HER*) Okay, I'm going to be pai--?

BEN. (*Interrupts*) You will be paid, Miss Peabody. For bringing us... a Katz Man. Come. I'm taking everybody out for a meal.

ARTHUR / YEWANDE. Blintzes?

BEN. Word up.

(*As THEY all start to go...*)

BEN. The one thing I don't get, Miss Peabody, is after searching New York, London, Spain and... Madrid... and riding a motor scooter, how did you find our brother right here?

SALLY. Honestly... I was visiting this temple in Encino and there's a bar next door. Lucky Joe's. In walks Yewande. We have a few rum and cokes, listen to a few songs on the jukebox, I pinch his ass, we hit it off, he tells me his life story. All I did was put two and two together. I got lucky.

BEN. I didn't think you went to Madrid.

ARTHUR. Maybe it's a *hekaya.*

BEN. WHAT THE HELL DOES THAT MEAN?

ARTHUR. Beats me!

YEWANDE. It means -- miracle.

(THEY all nod as THEY exit. LIGHTS FADE.)

THE BASIC 7

The living room of The Bromberg's.

BART BROMBERG, 30s, jiggles HIS keys outside, opens the door and runs in, in sheer delight. Practically skipping in and flailing arms wildly. He is all in black including a black ski cap, shirt, slacks and black Converse high-tops. HE clutches a "recycle" bag from a supermarket to HIS chest.

BART. This is the best thing that has ever happened to me. The best thing. The most wonderful, best, bestest best, unbelievably bestest best thing I could ever imagine.

(Enter, SHEILA. 30s, cute, in bright day-glow orange jump sweats and a humongous Star-of-David around HER neck. SHE is also on top of the world and also holds tightly to a matching bag.)

SHEILA. This is the best thing that has ever happened to me. The best thing. The most wonderful, best, *bestest* best, unbelievably *bestest* best thing I could ever imagine.

BART. *(Moving to HER)* How do you feel, Sheila?

SHEILA. How do I look like I feel?

BART. You look like you feel that this is the *bestest* best thing that you could ever imagine.

SHEILA. The most wonderful, best, *bestest* best, unbelievably *bestest* best thing I could ever imagine.

(THEY giggle like kids and scurry to the sofa.)

BART. When I count to three.

SHEILA. On three.

BART. I will count to three.

SHEILA. Are you doing one two three, and then we open the bags, or are you doing one two and *on three* we open the bags?

BART. Why do you do that?

SHEILA. Do what?

BART. Make things difficult? Why can't things be easy and carefree?

SHEILA. *(Mimics HIM)* I'm making things easy and carefree. What -- I'm making things difficult because I don't know if I should open the bag on three or *after* three? That's being difficult?

BART. Now I don't know if we're opening the bags on three or after three. You see what you did.

SHEILA. Let's not ruin this, Bart. We both worked so hard for this. We can't ruin it.

BART. *(Instructional)* Okay. I'll hold up three fingers and then we'll open the bag.

SHEILA. Am I waiting for the third finger to go up or are we opening the bag on the third finger?

BART. Why do you do that?

SHEILA. Do what?

BART. Confront everything I do. Why can't things be easy and carefree?

SHEILA. *(Mimics HIM)* I'm making things easy and carefree. And I'm confronting things because I don't know if I should open the bag on the third finger or after the third finger? That's confronting?

BART. OPEN THE BAG!

(SHEILA opens HER bag and pulls out a package of gum.)

BART. What is that?

SHEILA. Juicy Fruit.

BART. Juicy Fruit. That's what you got?

SHEILA. You said we could take anything we wanted. I wanted Juicy Fruit.

BART. Sheila, this was supposed to be dangerous and crazy. Sheila and Bart Bromberg walk into a market and steal something. STEAL SOMETHING.

SHEILA. I did. I stole Juicy Fruit. It's gum.

BART. I know it's gum! Who the hell wants gum? You were supposed to rob... to get the rush of taking something illegally... you were supposed to break a rule. That's what we're trying to do here, honey, break some rules.

SHEILA. Tell me again why wc want to break some rules?

BART. For greed, Sheila, that's what this is about. Giving the finger to the big man. *(HE uncharacteristically gives the index finger... then the middle finger)* Taking back something that was never ours to begin with. You know we've been living our lives much too safely.

SHEILA. You said if we did this, we would feel alive again.

BART. Out of our rut.

SHEILA. Look at us. Particularly you.

BART. Huh?

SHEILA. We're arguing over gum, Bart. This was just supposed to be an adventure, now we're fighting!

BART. Well you didn't take a good thing. The store won't even know it's missing. The whole point of this was to show ourselves that we can do something sinful. Wrong. We're too good, Sheila, we've been boring since the day we met.

SHEILA. I was boring the day before we met.

BART. We have a nice apartment.

SHEILA. We pay our rent on time.

BART. We both have secure jobs --

SHEILA. A pension for you --

BART. A 401K for you.

SHEILA. Boring people find us boring.

BART. This is greed, Sheila, greed in the best sense of the word.

SHEILA. *(Turned on)* This is robbery. Felony. Breaking and entering... ly.

BART. And we need to do more of it.

SHEILA. We should tell our friends.

BART. Go public.

SHEILA. What's the point of us just not being boring to each other? We should tell people.

BART. Spread the word. Sheila and Bart Bromberg are out there and you better watch out.

SHEILA. I liked the taste of it, Bart.

BART. The gum?

SHEILA. The feeling of being bad. *(SHE slaps HIS ass)* I know it's a sin and all...

BART. Your father the <u>rabbi</u> would have something negative to say about this for sure.

SHEILA. What about your father the congressman?

BART. Oh -- and your mother, the second grade school teacher voted best teacher in America, two years in a row?

SHEILA. Your sister works in a leper colony! *(Beat)* Yeah we shouldn't tell anyone.

BART. No. It's probably good enough we both know we're not boring anymore.

SHEILA. This is a slippery slope, Bart. We are talking one of the seven deadly sins here. First this and then... then...

BART. What do you think we're going to move on to -- gluttony? We can't do that. We're both on the Beverly Hills Diet.

SHEILA. Huu! *(SHE kisses the Star-of-David)* Oh thank goodness.

BART. We made the right decision. We don't want to get involved in the other deadly sins: Pride, envy, anger, lust, gluttony, and sloth. We picked a winner!

SHEILA. Especially if our other choice is sloth.

BART. It's the Seven Heavenly Virtues that's got us all screwed up.

SHEILA. Faith, hope, charity.

(SHE's stumped and looks at HIM for help. HE poses as if playing charades; muscles flexing.)

SHEILA. Fortitude.

(HE mimics the "Scales of Justice" sign.)

SHEILA. Justice.

The Bitter Herbs

(HE pretends to sip a cup of tea).

SHEILA. Temperance.

(HE holds HIS hands over HIS crotch.)

SHEILA. Penis!

BART. Prudence!

SHEILA. Prudence? YEAH!

(THEY high five).

BART. And we don't even know what prudence is but I'm sure it's screwed us up!

SHEILA. But we're greedy, Bart. We want what is not ours. Like Juicy Fruit.

BART. Well, Sheila, darling, we chose greed because it's a popular one. People swipe things all the time. It's natural. When you were a kid, didn't you... lift things now and again?

SHEILA. Don't be ridiculous.

BART. A chocolate bar from a local candy shop?

SHEILA. Absolutely not.

BART. What about a dollar from your mother's purse?

SHEILA. Huh--NEVER! *(SHE kisses the Star-of-David)* I once put two dollars into my mother's purse as a thank you for being a good mother. I was four.

BART. *Booooring.*

SHEILA. That is boring! Look at the horrible state we've gotten ourselves into. Particularly you.

BART. Huh? You keep saying that!

SHEILA. Well this was all your idea, Bart. I was perfectly fine being misses goody two-shoes. Ironically I only have two pairs of shoes since I thought having three fell into the category of lust.

BART. You have to stay strong, Sheila. This was the right thing for us.

SHEILA. No. No. Look. We're both not aging well. Particularly you.

BART. Sheila! Enough of this. Now, it was time for us to be a little greedy and that is why we made this pact.

SHEILA. For us.

BART. Our independence.

SHEILA. To challenge ourselves.

BART. To dare ourselves.

SHEILA. And that is why I stole the pack of Juicy Fruit.

BART. It's gum!

SHEILA. I know it's gum. Well what the hell did you steal, Mr. Greed Is My Business?

BART. *(Takes out of the bag some razor blades)* Here.

SHEILA. What is that? Razor blades?

BART. Don't be naive, Sheila. They're Gillette Mach 3 cartridges.

SHEILA.*(Laughing)* THAT'S what you stole? THAT'S your attempt at greed? Razor blades?

BART. Mach 3! Mach 3!

SHEILA. You're a child!

BART. Oh and gum? Gum is adult. Gum is supposed to show the world that Sheila and Bart Bromberg are a couple to contend with? While multi-national corporations and the oil industry are tearing down every fiber of good life we are trying to establish, it's the little man that gets taken, Sheila, the little man. I'm the little man. The tiny man. But no more, Sheila. This act of defiance directed straight on to the elite that is trying to keep us down is to show them that we are not going to take it any longer. Not a single day longer, my dear. Not one single second longer -- we are going to revolt! Revolution, Sheila, that is why we steal. *(HE waves an imaginary flag a la Les Miserables)* Our greed can be just as big as their greed, honey, just as big. They picked the wrong couple, Sheila. They thought we were boring but they were wrong. And gum... gum is BORING!

SHEILA. It's your favorite.

BART. What?

SHEILA. I stole the gum for you.

BART. You stole the gum for me?

SHEILA. Because it's your favorite.

BART. *(Looks at it closely)* Ohhh. I love Strappleberry.

SHEILA. When I walked into the store I was scared, Bart, I was scared. This was a big move for me, *waaay* beyond the Sheila Bromberg comfort zone. But then you made a beeline for pharmaceuticals and I had to make a decision. Sure I wanted to give it to the big man. *(SHE gives the index finger... then the middle finger)* For my little man. They should know they're overpricing us, and destroying the middle-class's way of life. *(SHE uncharacteristically gives the middle finger)* They have no right to charge these exorbitant prices while CEO's take golden parachutes and we're left scrounging to make ends meet. It's not fair to me as a person. A woman. A Bromberg! But then I got to thinking... we're actually not even suffering that much. Heck, We're not even middle-class. We go to Maui every summer. So then I just thought, I should just get something nice for my husband. Because I love him. Strappleberry Juicy Fruit.

BART. I feel foolish.

SHEILA. Because of how selfish the razor blades...

BART. Mach 3, Mach 3!!!

SHEILA. Because of how selfish the Mach 3's are in retrospect?

BART. I had my hand right on the tampons, for you...

SHEILA. You're forgiven. *(She kisses the Star-of-David. Then a new idea:)* If we return these items...

BART. HUU!

SHEILA. -- We'll be better than the multi-national corporations and oil industry.

BART. No. Not the Mach 3's! *(Thinks it over)* You're right. You're right we will be better than they are.

SHEILA. We'll bring them both back. And we go on with our lives. Our boring, staid, normal, comfortable, and yet... beautiful lives together.

BART. I guess we're stuck with faith, hope, charity, fortitude, justice, temperance, and prudence.

SHEILA. And we don't even know what prudence is but I'm sure it's screwed us up.

BART. We're also stuck with each <u>other</u>.

SHEILA. Is that so bad?

BART. You're the best thing that has ever happened to me. The best thing. The most wonderful, best, bestest best, unbelievably bestest best thing I could ever imagine.

(THEY kiss.)

The Bitter Herbs

SHEILA. Let's go.

(THEY start for the door.)

BART. You got a dollar on you?

SHEILA. No, why?

BART. Suddenly I'm dying for a piece of Juicy Fruit.

SHEILA. I'll stick it in my bra, they're so easy to steal.

(THEY put the stuff back in THEIR bags, laugh, and exit. BLACKOUT.)

JOIN THE CLUB

A living room in Santa Monica, California with modest furniture. There is an entrance in the right wall, and a kitchen area, up, left.

ESTHER ZULMAN, 30s, is fresh faced and nervous. SHE sits on a stool and reads the book: HOW TO BE CATHOLIC. SHE hears the door opening.

ESTHER. Bobby?

(BOBBY O'MALLEY, fair-skinned and Midwestern stands on the threshold. in a football jersey.)

ESTHER. Did you do it? Bobby, did you do i--?

(HE puts up HIS hand to stop HER and crosses the room bent over and hardly able to walk.)

BOBBY. -- You are so lucky I love you, Esther, you are more than lucky that I love you.

ESTHER. Did you do i--?

BOBBY. -- Oh I did it, Esther. Okay? I did it. You think I'm walking this way because I'm looking for loose quarters on the floor? I -- did -- it!

ESTHER. You -- did -- it. Oh, Bobby.

BOBBY. Would you like me to reenact the first incision to prove that I did it?

ESTHER. I believe you. Oh, Bobby.

BOBBY. Look in the car. There might be my tears all over the steering column and a dent in the dashboard where my fist was pounding the entire drive home. Will that prove to you that I did it? *(Off HER look as SHE gets emotional)* Oh, baby, I'm sorry.

ESTHER. *K'sheohavim low tschrim lomar 'Ani mitstaer.*

BOBBY. What?

ESTHER. It's Hebrew. "Love... is never having to say you're sorry."

BOBBY. Well just say it. Oh forget it. I did it. Now there's no reason to draw attention to any of it anymore.

(HE sits and SCREAMS wildly. SHE rushes to HIM...)

ESTHER. It must hurt.

BOBBY. Do me a favor, Esther. Go into the kitchen and close the oven door on your ears. That's how it hurts. Go into the garage and lower the half ton metal door on the softest part of your ankle.

ESTHER. It's just a procedure.

BOBBY. A procedure? NO, no Esther, a procedure is having a wisdom tooth pulled. A procedure is having carpal tunnel surgery. A procedure is even having out-patient inguinal hernia surgery! This is not a procedure, Esther. This was a sick, sick, sick thing that I had done to myself that should never be done to any other living human being. *(Notices)* You're crying?

(SHE wasn't, but now SHE is.)

BOBBY. Don't cry... Esther, don't cry. *(HE makes nice)* Better? *(SHE nods)* You'll be fine. *(SHE smiles)* All good now. HEY. Wait a second... I'm the one whose body's been crucified!

ESTHER. Bobby. You're getting carried away.

BOBBY. What do you call it when a thirty-four year old man has a... a... what did you call it?

ESTHER. A *bris.*

BOBBY. I was circumcised!

ESTHER. It was religious.

BOBBY. It was my *pee-pee*.

ESTHER. It's in the Old Testament.

BOBBY. A grown man took my favorite appendage and used a cheese grater on it -- are you sure that's in the Old Testament?

ESTHER. You are one step closer to my parents accepting you.

BOBBY. I want to die right here in the living room but we don't have circumcision insurance and you'll be left without a cent.

ESTHER. *Savlanout.*

BOBBY. What?

ESTHER. It's Hebrew. "Patience," Bobby

BOBBY. Well just say it. Oh forget it. I did it. Now there's no reason to draw attention to any of it anymore.

(HE sits and SCREAMS wildly. SHE rushes to HIM...)

ESTHER. It must hurt.

BOBBY. You want to make it better... make it not happen in the first place.

ESTHER. I don't know why you're treating me like this, Bobby. This was very important to my family. We're getting married in twelve months and we both agreed... we <u>both</u> agreed that we were going to learn more about each other's religious practices before taking our vows.

BOBBY. Yes. I thought you meant opening a bank account or investing in a condo in Florida.

ESTHER. Bobby. My parents are *Shomer Shabbos*. They believe in all the laws God sent down from Mount Sinai. And a few they made up themselves. I grew up in a Kosher home. I was sent to temple every Friday night *and* Saturday morning. And after my *Bat Mitzvah,* I spent four summers working and living on a Kibbutz. Now that's dedication.

(HE awkwardly shuffles to HER.)

BOBBY. Sunday Mass every weekend for me. I was an alter boy. Two trips a year to Vatican City. I actually had a sit down with the Pope himself. You forget, my father was a diplomat... we had connections. I took Holy Communion from that man and kissed his ring.

ESTHER: *(Slightly disgusted)* Do you know many people kiss that ring?

BOBBY: Religion is as important to me as it is to you. We both want to keep our beliefs strong in our future marriage. *(SHE sniffles. HE hugs HER)* Better? *(SHE nods)* You'll be fine. *(SHE smiles)* All good now. HEY. Wait a second... I'm the one who cut off part of his original equipment! Damn it!

ESTHER. Bobby. You're getting carried away.

BOBBY. Did you know it's supposed to be done on the eighth day after birth? You do realize that, don't you? I'm thirty-four years and fifty-two days too late!

ESTHER. That's why it cost extra.

BOBBY. THAT'S WHY IT HURTS! I don't know how kids take it. It's torture.

ESTHER. But the doctor put a little wine on your lips to deaden the pain, right?

BOBBY. That's supposed to help?

ESTHER. They did that for my baby brother.

BOBBY. A bottle of Scotch wouldn't have helped this pain.

ESTHER. What about the custom of holding the baby during the *bris?*

BOBBY. Is <u>that</u> supposed to help?

ESTHER. They did that for my baby br-- *(HE throws HER a look)* It's called the *sandak*. Did anybody hold you, Bobby?

BOBBY. *(Nods)* My HMO representative. He couldn't stop laughing.

ESTHER. That doesn't sound like a *sandak* at all.

BOBBY. The second I walked into the clinic people were staring at me. They were there for real problems. Kidney stones, and bladder infections... I was there for what they actually call -- Cosmetic Surgery.

ESTHER. You should have let me go with you. You're so stubborn.

BOBBY. A lovely girl was in the bed next to me. She was getting her beautiful C-cups enlarged to D's so that her dancing career could take off. She asked what I was having done. I wept.

ESTHER. Oooh! I went to temple this morning. Wanted to make this a special day for you, so I had a naming ceremony.

BOBBY. With tears streaming down my cheek, I told her while she was going up two sizes, I was coming down two sizes. I was humiliated.

ESTHER. The naming of the child is the most emotional part of many *bris* ceremonies. Ashkenazic-European Jews, of which I am one, have the beautiful tradition of naming after the deceased.

BOBBY. When they put me under, I distinctly heard the doctor say, "Too bad, it's a beauty."

ESTHER. So since I miss my grandfather so much, and since you had the circumcision today, I've renamed you to bring you closer to the Jewish faith. From now on you will be called Yehoshua ben Hamim Yerushalayim.

BOBBY. A beauty he called it... one of a kind -- Excuse me, what did you call me?

The Bitter Herbs

ESTHER. Yehoshua ben Hamim Yerushalayim.

BOBBY. You mean *Yeho…Heroshima…ben…Yeru…shalayim…*O'Malley?

ESTHER. Grand-poppy would be so honored.

BOBBY. Esther. I can't go around with that name.

ESTHER. Why not?

BOBBY. I can't pronounce it for one. And it's very.... Jewish.

ESTHER. What are you saying? You don't want to be half Jewish?

BOBBY. I do, I do want to be half Jewish. But I suppose not the half they chopped off me this morning.

ESTHER. *(Now in full cry)* What about all the things I've done for you? You think I liked watching the uncut version of "The Passion of the Christ?" I had to take three showers and a bath to wash that feeling off me.

BOBBY. Honey, it was the Romans that crucified Jesus, not the Jews.

ESTHER. I'm talking about the directing.

(The doorbell rings. THEY freeze.)

BOBBY. We need help, Esther.

ESTHER. What we need is guidance.

BOBBY. A sign from above that you and I are meant to be together.

ESTHER. Words from God himself.

(SHE opens the door and RABBI MEYERS to enter. A short man in suit with yalmuka; who is agitated.)

RABBI MEYERS. Jesus Christ -- my car just got front-ended into my back end!

ESTHER. Rabbi Meyers!

BOBBY. Who hit you?

(FATHER DEMETRIE enters. A regal man with collar and straight-back.)

FATHER DEMETRIE. Moshe, I didn't front-end you in the back end, you back-ended me in the front end.

BOBBY. Father Demetrie.

RABBI MEYERS. He's a liar. This man is a liar. How could I back-end you with my front-end, if I was moving forward?

FATHER DEMETRIE. He's impossible. You're impossible, Moshe. *(To the others)* He's impossible... Whenever I have to counsel with this man, he's impossible.

RABBI MEYERS. I get impossible when I'm front-ended into my back end.

FATHER DEMETRIE. You were parking your car. I was already parked. You back-ended me in the front end. I couldn't have hit you.

RABBI MEYERS. He's going to tell me about driving. I was driving already when you were still in seminary.

FATHER DEMETRIE. Don't talk to me about driving. I was on the Prefecture of the Economic Affairs of the Holy See that controlled all governing bodies. And we played Bumper Car. Beat the pants off Cardinal Hickey in the final turn for the checkered flag.

RABBI MEYERS. You didn't even have your lights on.

FATHER DEMETRIE. I just had Lasik Eye Surgery.

RABBI MEYERS. How are you, dear, Esther?

FATHER DEMETRIE. Bobby, it's good to see you, my son. *(HE slaps BOBBY on the back which doubles him over)*

RABBI MEYERS. *(Whispers to ESTHER)* He's not giving you any trouble, is he?

FATHER DEMETRIE. Why would Bobby give her trouble?

RABBI MEYERS. Why would Bobby give her trouble? I don't know why Bobby would give her trouble. Maybe it's because he's going to be scaring her half to death with the heaven, hell, purgatory story.

FATHER DEMETRIE. And the burning bush doesn't keep a boy up at night?

RABBI MEYERS. The burning bush story is an anecdotal piece about belief, and commitment to the Almighty.

FATHER DEMETRIE. It's also an allegory to put out forest fires.

RABBI MEYERS. You're impossible. And you can't drive.

ESTHER. Maybe we should all sit down.

RABBI MEYERS. Watch him. He'll probably back into your coffee table and send your sofa to the body shop. *(To ESTHER)* How are you, *dahling*? He's not putting pressure on you to give up your culture, your history or your *yiddish-kite, is he?*

FATHER DEMETRIE. Bobby wouldn't do that.

RABBI MEYERS. How do you know he wouldn't do that? If his faith is strong, and his belief divine, his wishes might overpower sweet Esther Zulman here and then one day I'd show up and find her crossing herself and taking Holy Communion over a plate of ham hocks and melted Gorgonzola. Speaking of which... Do you have a piece of fish, dear?

(ESTHER exits.)

RABBI MEYERS. I haven't eaten all day and the Brofman funeral went so long this morning, I thought Melvin was going to be reincarnated before we shoved the dirt.

FATHER DEMETRIE. You worry too much, Rabbi Meyers.

RABBI MEYERS. I don't mind worrying for the both of us. That's the tribe I belong to.

FATHER DEMETRIE. Catholics worry just as much. I was in the The Congregation for Divine Worship and the Discipline of the Sacraments where I worried about the future of our Holy Father and this Church so much, I beat the pants off Cardinal Keeler and received the award for "Most Worry Lines" in my face.

(ESTHER enters with drink and cookies.)

ESTHER. *Haeem coolanu low yicholeem lichiot b'shalom?*

(THEY all look at HER.)

ESTHER. It's Hebrew. "Can't we all just get along?"

(MEYERS looks at the food but doesn't take any.)

BOBBY. What she means is... we thank you both for coming today... we can't thank you enough for counseling us on our upcoming nuptials. Father, Rabbi. Esther and I know interfaith marriages have a very high percentage of failure.

FATHER DEMETRIE. Seventy-three percent.

RABBI MEYERS. Seventy-<u>five</u> percent!

ESTHER. We're willing to do anything...

BOBBY. Almost... <u>everything</u>.

ESTHER. *(Nods)* Everything.

BOBBY. *(Nods, nervously)* Everything...

FATHER DEMETRIE. Rabbi Meyers and I are delighted you have chosen us.

The Bitter Herbs

RABBI MEYERS. Your wedding is a year off -- we have plenty of time.

(HE reaches for a cookie...)

FATHER DEMETRIE. Before we begin...

(MEYERS doesn't get the cookie.)

FATHER DEMETRIE. Might I recite a *Novena of Petition.*

(THEY all rise, lower THEIR heads.)

FATHER DEMETRIE. OH LORD. My Jesus, You have said: "Truly I say to you, ask and it will be given you, seek and you will find, knock and it will be opened to you."

(The OTHERS start to sit, but HE goes on and THEY stand again. BOBBY in pain.)

FATHER DEMETRIE. Behold I knock, I seek and ask for the grace of this upcoming marriage and pray for Bobby O'Malley and Esther Zulman -- Sacred Heart of Jesus, I place all my trust in You! O my Jesus. Amen.

BOBBY. Amen.

(About to sit...)

FATHER DEMITRIE. Would you like to say anything, Rabbi?

(THEY stand again...)

RABBI MEYERS. Yes. I could use that fish now.

(ESTHER exits. THEY sit. BOBBY flinches.)

FATHER DEMETRIE. Bobby. What's wrong?

BOBBY. *(Leans HIS head on DEMETRIE)* I'm shattered, Father Demetrie. I'm broken. I had a circumcision this morning.

RABBI MEYERS. *Bris?*

ESTHER. *(Pokes HER head in)* Because we love each other.

BOBBY. *(Through gritted teeth)* She does things for me too.

FATHER DEMETRIE. What did you do, Bobby?

RABBI MEYERS. Circumcision has been a part of our chronicle for five thousand seven hundred and sixty-seven years and I've never heard of one single case where the participant wanted his snippet back.

BOBBY. *(Gently raises HIS hand)* I want mine back.

ESTHER. *(Enters with a bowl of fruit)* Bobby!

FATHER DEMETRIE. Mixed marriages are not easy to maneuver through. This kind of decision should be discussed in detail.

RABBI MEYERS. Not too much detail I hope. I'm gonna be eating soon.

(MEYERS looks at the food, but just shakes HIS head.)

FATHER DEMETRIE. Why did you to do this to yourself, Bobby?

BOBBY. *(Accusatorial)* Her!

ESTHER. Bobby! He's just in pain, that's why the mood.

RABBI MEYERS. I think it was a very nice thing to do. *(Off)* If you're a *schmuck.*

ESTHER. But, Rabbi, I also went to temple and did a naming ceremony.

RABBI MEYERS. Now that's wonderful. What did you go with?

ESTHER. Yehoshua ben Hamim Yerushalayim.

RABBI MEYERS. O'Malley's going to have one hell of a letterhead.

FATHER DEMETRIE. Let's not make them nervous, Moshe.

RABBI MEYERS. Sometimes serious religious debate gets to the truth, Father Demetrie.

FATHER DEMETRIE. You don't think I don't know that. I've argued with the best at the Supreme Tribunal of the Apostolic Signatura -- disputing for Justice in the Church. Beat the pants off Cardinal Szoka to the point...

MEYERS/DEMETRIE... *he took ill.*

RABBI MEYERS. Is anyone in that church of your still <u>wearing</u> their pants?

BOBBY. *(Beat)* We thought sharing religions was the best way to go.

ESTHER. Yeah. You see... you see we know a lot about each other's religion. "One who denies that Christ is God cannot become His temple of the Holy Spirit." Letters 73:12. *(SHE turns to BOBBY and motions)*

BOBBY. Nobody ever celebrates Purim because they don't know what the hell to do.

RABBI MEYERS. No, no, children... the idea is not to just cram this information down. You have to figure out what it means to you. What God means to you.

ESTHER. Wait a moment. Are you saying I didn't have to learn how to genuflect and cross myself?

RABBI MEYERS. *(Off)* Oye.

FATHER DEMETRIE. Religion's symbols and rituals are learned over time... it's what's in your soul that matters.

BOBBY. So I didn't have to put on that *teffilin* thing in the morning and tie myself up like a mummy?

RABBI MEYERS. Why would you? You don't have any respect for it yet. You have no reference point to bring it into your daily life.

ESTHER. I wore an Easter Bonnet for a solid day. *(Breaks down)* And it was the first night of Passover!

(BOBBY staggers over to HER.)

BOBBY. Yeah, lady, well I built a *Sukkot* in the backyard. She made me build it. I don't even know why I built it. I threw my back out and needed four stitches in my head when I built that darn thing. She didn't have to make me build it. And she certainly didn't have to make it a two story.

ESTHER. I celebrated *Lent,* buster! Lent!

BOBBY. Hey. Lent is a season of soul-searching, reflection, and repentance. What the hell did Hanukkah get me?!

ESTHER. It gave you eight presents for eight solid days -- you selfish bitch!

BOBBY. Woa! Jesus killer!

ESTHER. THERE IS NO SANTA CLAUS!

BOBBY. *(To Demetrie, sotto)* Father... Is this true?

RABBI MEYERS. Children, please... we need to find calm.

FATHER DEMETRIE. *(Exploding)* Look at the two of you -- *chavers*. Don't be so *fartoost*. You're getting me all *oysgeshpilt* with your fighting. This is turning into a big *shtunk* and I won't have it. Now let's not let this *shtuss* happen. Esther is a lovely *bren,* and Yehoshua is a patient *mench*. And you're both *hocking me a tshynik. Oy Gotenyu,* you love each other so much you were willing to completely change for each other. The rabbi and I came here today just to *kvell* over you. And what do we find? This whole wedding *magillah* blowing up in your faces and you're both full of *dreck* -- and you still have a year to go! *(To BOBBY)* And you're a *putz* for doing the ol' snip-snip on the little fella! Now I'm going to give you both the *emess*. You want the *emess*, I'm going to give you the *emess*. *(As Jack Nicholson)* You can't handle the *emess*. The *emess* means *gornish* if you both have the same religion but don't have love. You two have love: *Kina-hora*. And if there is true love, why should religion get in the way? It's *nisht gut*. No good!

You can't become each other, you can only come together and be as one in the universe of God. Whether it's his God or her god... *nisht geferlich.* I once saw a Baptist try to marry a Muslim. *Gevalt!* My point is; religion is supposed to bring us close together, and the two of you have done nothing but tear yourselves apart. It's a *shanda. Now* I want the two of you to look each other in the eyes... *punim to punim...* and see if there is going to be a marriage here. And *es gezunterheyt. (HE sits)*

RABBI MEYERS. *(Long pause, to FATHER)* You're *gooood.*

FATHER DEMETRIE. A *shtikl.*

RABBI MEYERS. You know... you're not so impossible.

FATHER DEMETRIE. *Schmoozing* with you has taught me a little something.

RABBI MEYERS. *(Rises)* "And he said to them, "Why are you afraid, O men of little faith?" Then he rose and rebuked the winds and the sea; and there was a great calm."

FATHER DEMETRIE. Rabbi? That's Matthew 8-26.

RABBI MEYERS. I don't even know how I know that *mishegas.*

FATHER DEMETRIE. I know how you know. The same way these children should learn about each other. Not because their parents are putting some pressure on them to share a religion. But because they're best friends.

RABBI MEYERS. Like you and me.

FATHER DEMETRIE. Like you and me. It's osmosis. God moves about through all peoples.

RABBI MEYERS. Except the radicals.

FATHER DEMETRIE. Not the radicals.

ESTHER. Oh, Bobby.

BOBBY. *(The same way:)* Oh, Esther. We have been going about this the wrong way.

ESTHER. *(SHE looks around the room)* You think? Honey. Perhaps after the *sukkot* incident it was wrong of me to press for circumcision.

BOBBY. I shouldn't have been so forceful about baptizing you in the Jacuzzi.

ESTHER. Anyone can recover from water in the lungs. *(SHE coughs)*

BOBBY. Better? You'll be fine. All good now.

RABBI MEYERS. It's just religion. It doesn't have to make you crazy.

ESTHER. I'm sorry about Santa.

BOBBY. *(Throws a look at DEMETRIE)* Let's not talk about it.

RABBI MEYERS. *(To DEMETRIE)* You know, we should exchange insurance cards.

FATHER DEMETRIE. Why? I didn't front-end you in the back end, you back-ended me in the front end.

RABBI MEYERS. How could I back-end you in the –

FATHER DEMETRIE. -- Eh, the car belongs to the Parish anyway. Let them pay. Come on. I'll take you out for dinner.

RABBI MEYERS. I never did get that fish.

(THEY exit.)

ESTHER. We're on the right track now, Bobby. We're going to buck the trend of interfaith marriages that end in divorce.

BOBBY. And respect each others religious peculiarities.

ESTHER. *(Looks at HIM)* I love you, Yehoshua ben Hamim Yerushalayim

The Bitter Herbs

O'Malley.

BOBBY. I love you Esther… *Yero…Hero…* Zulman O'Malley.

(THEY kiss.)

BOBBY. Ooh. I gotta run. I have Bar Mitzvah practice in an hour.

(HE starts to go and screams in pain. BLACKOUT)

Other Plays by Mark Troy

The Secret Nymph of New Hyde Park
(6m 3f.)
A New York Senator finds out his wife has some extra political activities in order to raise money for his run. "'The Secret Nymph' is a wild and woolly romp… go along with a gag, a giggle or a guffaw (in this) zany sex farce and savvy political satire whipped together into a froth of frenzied absurdity." Drama-Logue

Tsuris
(4m 5f.)
Retirement in Century Village never looked so *facocked* when two lovers meet only to find out their aging parents are having an affair. "Comic tribulations aplenty... over-the-top orgy of Borscht-Belt-flavored slapstick." IN-Magazine Los Angeles

Paging Dr. Chutzpah
(2m 3f.)
Psychiatrist Lester Oronofsky is New York's most disreputable doctor… and now he has to train his own nephew in his footsteps. "A saucy boulevard romp. A lewd and lunatic study that kicks the Catskills style into a place somewhere between Woody Allen and Hooters. Troy has a talent for outsized patter, and he certainly layers on the situational dynamics." Los Angeles Times

Belladonnas of the Court
(3m 3f).
When a local L.A. neighborhood is scheduled for demolition, the inhabitants must band together to save what little community pride they have. "Mark M Troy's modernistic reflections on gentrification in LA's Fairfax District commands respect with Ionesco style banter…. It's refreshing." LA Weekly

Desperation
(1m 3f.)
Debbie Zlotnik has no idea what she is getting herself into when she is coupled with Gerald Febermiltz after joining the Insta-Mating Dating Service. It's only a matter of time before she finds out that Gerald has murdered the previous two women the dating service has sent over. "'Desperation' displays a remarkable adroit use of language and characterization in the ingenious exploration of male/female relationships." Village View

About the Author

Mark Troy has had over 50 plays produced around the world that include: New York; *Desperation* (Samuel French), *The Plot* (Riant Festival), *Jewel Avenue* (Writer's Theater), *Aggravation* (Theatre-Studio). *Los Angeles; Tsuris, Paging Dr. Chutzpah* (Sidewalk Studio Theatre), *Belladonna's of the Court* (Theatre League, Best Comedy), *The Secret Nymph of New Hyde Park* (Renegade Theater), *Peking Duck* (Next Stage), *Homewrecker* (Rose Theatre), *Figment* (American Globe, NYC). Regional; *The Proposal* (Actors Theatre of Louisville), *Balloon* (Chicago Dramatist Winner), *Getting You Bupkus,* (Malibu Stage Company), *Everyone I know* (L.A. Short Play Festival Winner), *Sister Snell* (Acme, Boston), *How To Marry Your Stalker,* (Harrogate, England), *Man on the Mountain* (British Columbia). Troy is the winner of the Claire Donaldson Prize For Playwrighting with his play *Afterpiece.* He co-wrote the feature film *Driving Me Crazy* starring Mickey Rooney and Celeste Holm and also wrote the cult classic *Zipperface.* He teaches screenwriting and is a member of the WGA and The Dramatist Guild. He lives in Los Angeles with the love of his life, playwright/actress Colette Freedman, and his greyhound Moses. www.curtainrise.com

www.ingramcontent.com/pod-product-compliance
Lightning Source LLC
Chambersburg PA
CBHW021345090426
42742CB00008B/759